I Am Amazing: Wisdom, Poetry & Affirmations

By April Dishon Barker

To everyone who has forgotten their worth:
You are amazing!

Contents

About the Author

Honor is a word that the Lord has recently laid on my heart. To be honorable is to be held to a very high standard, to be looked up to, to be inspirational. Honor is what we are to show God and His people. It is the very base of our faith as Christians. Jesus showed the utmost Honor to everyone around him and most of all, to His Father.

Honor is the word I think of when April Barker comes to my mind. April has been an instrumental inspiration to me from the moment we became co-workers years ago; selfless servitude, graceful kindness, and deep empathy for others are what make April who God made her to be. He has beautifully intertwined honor into each of these graceful qualities. April is a woman of honor, which is not an easy task to take on.

I am filled with excitement as April journeys through the pages of this book with us. May it help us grow closer to the Lord while learning how to best honor Him.

Natalie Pirrone
Education and Outreach Director, Poiema Foundation/ fighting Human Trafficking

A Note from the Author

Here I am and here it is. A book filled with the sincere and unabashed love, support, encouragement, empowerment, and affirmation that you never knew you needed but your soul has been waiting for.

I struggled for years wondering why my pure-hearted love, support, loyalty and acts of kindness were rejected and misunderstood so often. I had to come to realize that I was pouring in the wrong place. I noticed that the hearts that needed it, would always receive it with joy.

"I Am Amazing", is about my journey to choose joy every day. It touches on my story while using discretion. Writing it gave me the necessary reminder that I am most joyous when I am bringing joy to others.

The wisdom in this book is a compilation of things I have written, thought, or spoken in the last decade. The poetry is an outpour of my heart from life experiences of myself and/or others. The affirmations are words of encouragement, empowerment, or prophecy that I have released over the years to a smaller audience and now to more of the world.

Retrieve, receive and believe the strength and soberness to come into agreement with the truth about yourself and say, "I Am Amazing!"

PART ONE: POETRY

I'm Still Me

I'm still me,
Can't you see?
I gained some weight.
Cleaned too many plates.
It was all the stress,
The marriage, work, bills and grown-up life mess.
The firing, the wiring of
Hush and pray
Never say,
Cuz, huh nobody cares, anyway!
I'm still me
Just bigger
 But not better
Feeling alone and pillowcase wetter
Food was my company
Three times a day, times an hour
Yes, the midnight hour.
Eat and pray, then snack a little
And the midnight snack
Became a midnight life
Hiding underneath the layers of my comfort food

Accumulated armor of burgers, fried chicken, ice cream
and coffee,
Iced please.
The bigger I became,
The more people forgot my name,
My value, my true self
Because Fat equals stealth.
I kind of like being invisible
So....
Is this the new me?
Nah, I don't think so.
I'm still me
Alive & Free
Watch me move
Watch me lose
Watch me chose
To be better!

I' Can't

I can't because I'm too poor.
I can't because I'm too broke.
I can't because I'm black.
I can't because I'm single.
I can't because I'm too young.
I can't because I don't make enough money.
I can't because he/she left me.
I can't because I gotta' raise these kids.
I can't because they never taught me that.
I can't because I don't learn fast.
I can't because she lied on me.
I can't because they won't pay me what I am worth.
I can't because I'm too tired.
I can't!
I just, I just can't
I absolutely CAN NOT!
Or, can I?

The Railing

Last picked
Left Out
Finger Flicked
Lip Pout
Furrowed Brows
Tight Eyes
I am mad, angry, absolutely enraged!
You get on my nerves,
I'd fire you if you already didn't get paid.
You eat like a horse,
You're as big as a house.
Stay out the kitchen
Stop stuffing your mouth!
Can't wait until you're 18,
So you can hurry up and GET OUT!

The Response

How can I be great if nobody wants me around?
I have a gift to sing, but nowhere to release the sound.
Why was I born?
When can I die?
If I did,
Would anyone even cry?
I want to leave as bad as they want me to,
 But have no plan B.
I wish they never laid down together,
It's not my fault they made me.
No compliments, no encouragement.
Just nagging,
Tongues wagging and
Critical words that cut like a knife.
I guess I will quit before I start,
But deep down inside I'm torn apart.
Should I keep trying to be seen,
By eyes that won't even look up from their telephone screen?
Abandoned,
Neglected.
Ridiculed,

Rejected.
Why should I try,
When can I die?

The Redemption

My child, I love you.
I think you're Amazing.
I know the hairs on your head
And when they'll start graying.

I made you in my image,
Gave you good and perfect gifts.
I have no shadow of a doubt,
Whatever you target you won't miss.

I am always with you,
Love you so much,
I went to Calvary and
Gave my life up.

I knew you were worth saving,
Believe Me it's true,
So don't live like I'm a liar,
Live like I love you!

Saved, Single and Satisfied

Jesus is my husband,
my books are my companions,
I sleep alone and snore quite loudly.
I cook for one,
clean when I'm done
and enjoy my peace profoundly.

When the time is right,
I trust and know,
That God has a spouse for me.
He will love my Shake & Bake chicken,
Then happily wash the dishes,
Because they upset my allergies.

We will have two or three children,
Who will look like him and act like me,
And never talk back or disobey.
They will do well in school,
Eat all their veggies and
Do their chores before I even say.

Marriage, Mommies and Miracles

Okay, okay, I admit I was mistaken,
Twenty years of marriage and four kids later
My truth was flipped and shaken.

The shake and bake didn't make the cut very long,
Dishes don't wash themselves and
When I did them, I wasn't whistling a song.

Church, chicken and children,
That's all our young marriage could afford at first
We lived off Love, laughter and folding clothes 'til our hands hurt.

Books were replaced with dirty diapers
And suspicious moments of silence.
As for schoolwork, I couldn't help with math and barely could help with science!

As you can see, from single to now,
My head quickly came down out of the clouds.
At night when I pray I say, Lord have your way,
I think I hear Him laughing out loud.

I Am Amazing!

I am amazing!
I say it to remember.
When the world is too big
Game of life is too rigged
When I'm falling like a tree after "Timber!"

I am amazing!
I have to repeat.
When the job loss is real,
Car repo not a steal
And for lunch I have no money to eat.

I am amazing!
I try not to forget,
How I'm wonderfully made,
No bragging no shade
God spoke it, it's true on that you can bet. (Well, you shouldn't though)!

I am Amazing!
I tell you the truth,
I laugh and I smile
Walk by faith mile by mile
Cuz' in Christ I can't lose.

I am Amazing.
And I'm just getting started,
I'm blessing not stressing
God's Words I'm confessing
Professing promises to the pure hearted.

Yes! I am Amazing.
I am Amazing.
I am Amazing.
Cuz' God is Amazing!

PART TWO: WISDOM

Vision

It starts as a child. The dreams, ideas and creative expressions. Depending on the time taken by parents and teachers to listen to children and help them develop their gifts, we can see our children at all ages and stages of their lives living out their God-given destinies. It is never too early, and it is never too late to help a child write their vision. Or to help the child-like faith in you to dream, write out yours. In our family we do this twice a year. During Christmas break and at the end of the school year.

1. Write the vision.
2. Make a vision board.
3. Articulate it before a loving audience of close family and/or friends.
4. Put it up where you can see it every day.
5. See it. Speak it. Do it.

Humility

Just when you think you have learned the lesson of humility, something happens to make you realize it is a lifelong lesson that is never fully realized, only reinforced. When it is your turn to be humble, remember that you can make the decision to do so yourself or let God do it for you. Choose wisely.

Prepare for Promotion

My prayer for us all is that we do not allow fear to stop us from taking the opportunities that have been offered to us. I have prayed for many people's promotion. I know that some of them have been afforded opportunities to be promoted, but they wouldn't take it.

Fear paralyzed them. I pray that fear does not stop you from moving on, moving forward and moving up.

May we walk by faith and not by sight. May we see what God sees in us and believe in the ability to do all things through Christ who strengthens us. May we walk in power.

Here are three prophetic words that God gave me to speak over people in 2017 that changed their lives as they applied them consistently. These were given to me by God and are "Keys to the Kingdom" on how to access promotion and must be unlocked one at a time, over time.

Prophetic Declarations Regarding Promotion:

"As you increase your intimate time of intercession, God is going to promote you."

"As you increase your intimate time of intercession, God is going to give you houses and land."

"As you release your intimate time of intercession, God is going to make you a millionaire."

W.O.R.D.- Wisdom Occurs by Reading Daily

For all those out there trying to make things happen, (self-employed, on commission, etc.), don't get too busy for Him and His Word. Have you read your Bible today? What a difference the Word makes. He is never too busy for you. Read a chapter of the Bible, a Proverbs perhaps. Then say a quick prayer and get back on the grind.

After the Snow Melts

In February 2021 we had a major power outage in Texas on top of being snowed in. Here is a reflection that I had about that time.

After the snow, my heart is lighter, and I will continue to love without limits unconditionally. I am thankful that while I was cold externally and used blankets and clothing to warm myself, He let the fire of His truth and love melt the frozen places of my heart.

This week, while the snow was firmly packed all around our home with no sign of melting and blocking me from things I wanted to do, God was accessing the blocked-in places of my heart and mind melting the frozen thoughts I had about people. People who have said and done mean things this past year towards me, about me and people who look like me. People who spoke words of harsh judgement, grouping me in categories because of my skin and excluding me from their lives abruptly.

He melted my heart to show me that even though I forgave, I hadn't allowed Him to heal me of the wounds. The holes left in my heart where their friendship, conversations and past memories were drilled deep through the revelations of how they really felt about me and how easily they discarded me from their lives. There were SO many who did this that it was overwhelming.

The disrespect and disregard led to great discouragement. What was shocking is that I didn't even know I felt this way because I had glossed over it with the Christian duty to pray about it and forgive. God, however, showed up and revealed to me that which each change in relationship, He invites growth and wholeness. With each removal of a person's presence, there is more space for Him.

He didn't take the hurt, He allowed me to feel the pain, the rejection and sadness. Then He replaced it with the revelation of its purpose. The mercy of acceptance and the joy of deep and lasting forgiveness that produces the miracle of unconditional love, which is true freedom. This work allows me to allow Him to develop, (and in SOME instances redevelop), friendships and connections that look like His.

Whew- freedom. A freedom I didn't even know that I needed.

Plants & Personal Growth

Plants have changed my life perspective and enriched my purpose. Seeing in plants the type of growth that can happen when you nurture something daily is a reminder to me to stay still and let God love and nurture me. As I do so, I continue to grow and bring other people who are watching me the same joy I receive from my plants.

1. Buy a plant that looks beautiful to you. I love the Fiddle Leaf Fig Trees.
2. Find a pot that matches your home décor.
3. Read about how to care for it, (maybe do that before you buy it).
4. Name it! My Fiddle Leaf names are Frank, (after my grandfather) and Francesca.
5. Speak to it every morning and throughout the day.
6. Sing to it.
7. Buy a spray bottle and shower its leaves with water and water its roots as needed.
8. Watch it grow.

9. Replant in a BIGGER and BETTER space when it gets too big.

10. Remember to do all of the above for yourself!

Tears Should be Temporary

There is a time to cry. Tears are necessary at times.

Here are some important things to remember when crying and implement to end the crying season:

1. Make sure that you can trust the shoulder that you are crying on.

2. Do not look to people to make you feel better.

3. There really is only One who promises to wipe away EVERY tear.

4. When you are finished crying, pray for joy.

5. Dance. Yes, rejoice that you made it through a crying season. Seal the end of it with a dance of victory signifying very specifically that your time of crying is over.

6. Repeat as necessary.

Worship

I love the fact that our worship gets God's attention. In the presence of the Lord there is fullness of joy and treasures evermore. Whatever you do, do not let your worship go. It is a strategy against the plans of the devil. He flees at your worship. Heaviness lifts, sadness leaves with your worship. Joy comes, victory comes, truth comes. I pray that each and every day, you take time to worship.

Joy is a Discipline

This is a personal message to those who are downcast. I want to encourage you that joy is a discipline that can be practiced. Will you take a moment and smile? Now stretch those lips a little wider and show those teeth. Yes, that's it. Smile.

Feeling like you have nothing to smile about? Please humor me and get a pen and paper. Now let's play the opposite game. Everything that you are sad about, write down the opposite and smile.

Ex.

- Lost your job? Opposite- Next job will be doing something you love and would do for free.
- Feeling lonely? Opposite- Talk out loud to God like He is right next to you, because He is.
- He won't yell at you, lie to you, or make you feel bad. He is a really good listener.
- Worried about tomorrow? Opposite- Enjoy today. Do something for yourself.

Still not feeling it? I understand. I am giving you a reading hug and praying that the heaviness in your heart lifts swiftly in Jesus' name. God loves you; I love you. Those are the facts.

Live Out Your Faith not Your Emotions

Repent if you have allowed your emotions to get the best of you. I can't share the full details of how I went on a ride in anger around the city one day. I was looking for someone that had wronged me and almost made a permanent decision based on a temporary situation. I share that not to give you a dramatic visual but to say, it ain't always just prayer going on with Sis. April, okay?

I had to repent that day for what I was ABOUT to do. I repent every day for what I think and feel that doesn't lineup with the Word of God. Sin separates and I need to stay close to Him.

Read your Bible. I can tell when I haven't been spending enough time in the Word, my speech lacks faith and my emotions get the best of me. I do not produce or perform well during the day. I am easily frustrated and impatient.

We cannot spend more time reading traumatizing news, hate-filled social media posts, or even watching movies and listening to music than reading God's Word. What goes in will come out. Read your Bible and watch your viewpoint and attitude change daily.

Pray. Tell God how you feel FIRST not last. (I have struggled with the 'tell God first' first part of this off and on). Once you talk to Him about everything, you not only feel better, but you respond better. Sometimes, you don't even need to tell anyone else.

Share your testimony. Out of everything we post online or talk to people about offline, do we lift up Jesus? Do we offer hope? Prayer? Invite people to church? Do people even know we are believers? Satan's plan is to silence your love and faith in Jesus. Do not partner with that.

Today share with someone about Jesus. Lift up His Name and people will be drawn to the Him in you.

Perseverance

Keep going, even if you are uncomfortable, especially if you are uncomfortable. A couple of weeks ago I was experiencing several deep emotions while pondering a couple of long-term fiery trails that I was walking through.

I asked the Lord, "Why is all of this happening?"

The response was very matter-of-fact, "You have to go through these things in order to go to the next level."

I really was surprised to hear the voice of the Lord so clearly, not because He never speaks to me in that way, but because His response was so matter of fact and quick. I was walking about the house not even in a "prayer time". I was just going about the sweet communion of my day.

I felt this further explanation from God that was more of an impression than a conversation. The impression was this, "You can go through these fiery trails well and proceed to the next level, or you can opt out and stay on the level you are on."

When presented with this opportunity, some may have opted like the rich man to stay at his level of comfort and religion. I knew in that moment that I had no other option but to continue to walk with God through the fire. I have to say that the walk has been more bearable with the revelation of what was happening.

Elevation at a cost. One expense is the revelation of shallow, surface-level relationships. You know, the ones that only last when you are on the up and up. The people who speak to you when you are dressed nice. The ones who want the "fun" version of you. The "successful" version of you. The "trial-free version."

While losing these types of people from your life because of God's desire to elevate you doesn't feel nice, remember your elevation is not about them not being a good friend, or even being a "hater". It is more about His desire to be your only source of assurance, comfort and closest and most faithful friend.

There were many biblical good-byes. Abraham, Moses, David, Esther, Ruth, and yes, Jesus. The disciples then and disciples today like you and me, must all go through this experience on some level.

Remember that there is a burning bush, a midnight wrestling, a mountain top experience for every believer. Your elevation will be lonely but there is a friend that sticks closer than any brother. His name is Jesus and He is all you need.

The Midnight Hour

For those of us who have died to our will. (Gal. 2:20) For those of us who have put our hands to the plow and won't turn back. For those of us who are suffering for His names' sake.

Sometimes, you just have to moan. Late in the evening, when the sun is going down and your soul is weary; call upon the Lord and He will answer and give you peace, like a river.

Every once in a while, you have to sacrifice sleep and pray in the new day. Give God a "late in the midnight hour" prayer request and get a "joy in the morning" praise report!

Hallelujah!

"The Ten-Minute Commitment"

1. Sing a song. (No music, just sing from your heart straight to God's.) If you don't know one, an easy song is "Jesus Loves Me".

2. Say a Scripture. It doesn't have to be a whole chapter; it could be a verse you learned as a child or one you saw online last week. A great one is Psalm 23:1 "The Lord is my Shepherd; I shall not want."

3. Make a Supplication: the action of asking for something earnestly and humbly. First off, start by praying for the daily needs of your immediate family. Then, you can move on to extended family, and finally to friends. I can make a really long list of things to pray for, but for now, start there consistently.

4. Make sure you end your prayer, "In Jesus' name, Amen."

That's it! Will you answer the call to pray daily? Start with 10 minutes once a day and grow from there. It will be one of the best decisions you have ever made.

PART THREE: AFFIRMATIONS

Affirmations

Affirmation- to build up with words spoken repeatedly and consistently with a heart full of faith and a voice filled with power and conviction.
April Dishon Barker

In this section, you can speak these words over yourself by speaking in first person. You can speak them over loved ones by declaring them out loud. They originally came from the stirring of the Spirit of the Lord to me and I give them to you. Be affirmed and know that you are Amazing!

You are not irrelevant. You are irreplaceable. Never forget, there is only one you. Everything you touch has a fingerprint like no other. Use your hands with skill. Everywhere you walk has your footprint that cannot be duplicated. Walk with purpose. There is only one set of teeth like yours. Speak with wisdom.

April Dishon Barker

A Total Recovery

I prophesy that at the moment you read this you are entering a season of recovery:

Mental recovery is yours and you will no longer have a double mind. You will no longer be tormented by thoughts of what is happening on the other side of 'that' mountain, but you are visualizing 'that' mountain being picked up and cast into the sea. I decree that as you read the Word of God found in the book of James your mind is being renewed by the power that lies in the Holy Scripture.

Emotional recovery is yours and you will no longer be on an emotional roller coaster of bitterness and unforgiveness. Today you will declare that whatever they did or didn't do, whatever they said or didn't say, is forgiven and under the heart-healing blood of Jesus. Forgive now and forgive daily when the enemy tries to remind you of what was done to you and tell him, "Satan, it's under the blood!" Then, walk daily and nightly in the peace of God knowing that He will handle your enemies and heal every hurt.

Spiritual recovery is yours as you worship the King. Lift your hands and say,

"Lord, I repent for placing _____, (fill in the blank of the person, activity, item that has become an idol), on the throne of my heart and giving thoughts of them/it my time and emotional energy. Jesus, you alone died for me and gave me your Spirit. You gave me joy and victory. I am Yours and You are mine, I am walking in victory every day.

Today, I give You my heart again and I will let nothing, or no one ever take your place as King of my heart and Lord of my life. I worship you now and all the days of my life. Thank you for the blessing of salvation and I receive now every spiritual blessing that you have for me in Jesus' name, Amen."

The fullness of recovery that you have just been given will give you a testimony so great your loved ones will be saved and your co-workers will know that your God IS God! Amen and amen!

I am Covered

I speak a blessing today that the blood of Jesus Christ our Lord cover you and your family and keep you safe from hurt, harm and danger. That your spirit is stirred with a desire to be in God's presence and that you see the salvation of the Lord in every situation that you face. I speak comfort to the mourning, relief for the distressed, strength to the weary. Be lifted now in the name of Jesus! Amen and amen!

I Humble Myself Daily

Just when you think you have learned the lesson of humility something happens to make you realize it is a lifelong lesson that is never fully realized, only reinforced. So, while I am being taught, I will stay in peace of mind and a joy-filled heart radiating the love of Christ while I learn and learn and learn the lesson of humility. I humble myself.

I am Fearless

May God's perfect love cast out all fear. May you be overwhelmed by God's faithfulness today and every day. You are cherished and special to God and to me. God loves you, I love you.

I am Burden and Carefree

May the hope of heaven lift every burden and your day be filled with the abundant peace found only in knowing and loving Jesus with your whole heart. May the fall breezes calm your anxious heart as you enjoy daily fellowship with the One who causes the wind to blow. Rest in the Lord and all His promises.

I am Successful

I am about to blow up. My business is booming. God's hand of favor is upon me and I am walking through open doors that will allow me to be debt-free and break every spirit of poverty off of my family forever. Every meeting I have is led by the Holy Spirit and I speak with the wisdom and knowledge of a ruler. I am blessed in the city and the field. Favor follows me. Rich and wealthy people want to do business with me and invest in my business and/or partner with my ministry. I am good ground to give to and all those that bless me will be blessed. My children will be millionaires and walk with the Lord all the days of their lives. God's gracious hand is upon them. Health and wealth are the fruit of my spouse's labor and they daily walk upright before the Lord. Prayer is my access and I access it all in prayer. I am blessed bountifully and eternally. No one or nothing has the power to hinder my blessings and God's plans for me, my spouse nor my children. All power belongs to God. Amen and amen.

A Morning Prayer of Agreement for the Day

Lord,

This day I receive the mind of Christ instead of the mind of self. I believe the truth and not the lies. I will walk in joy and not discouragement. The works of my hands are blessed as I stay focused and refuse all distractions. I am more than able to do all that you have purposed me to do, with excellence and a smile. The enemy is defeated and all who he tries to use to block my path, progress and promotion are powerless and ashamed for trying to thwart God and His plan for me. I thank you for waking me up and giving me life. Use me for your glory and bless me abundantly with all that I have need of today. In Jesus' name. Amen.

Speak Life

As we commit to changing negative mindsets let's be mindful of what we say. Also, pray and ask God to forgive you for any words spoken in doubt, fear or disbelief. You will have what you say. Speak the truth, speak the Word of God, (scriptures), and speak life. Encourage, equip, edify, engage heavenly angels on your behalf. Your tongue has the power of life and death. Speak life!

☐

I am at Peace

Have you ever had a spectacular day and then all of a sudden, bam, it happens? Traffic on the way home from work, an argument with your spouse over something trivial. Maybe you are at peace and all of a sudden find yourself being overwhelmed with thoughts of something you are praying about that hasn't changed.

One small discomfort and the last 8 hours of walking in the fruit of the Spirit is null and void. This is a trick of the enemy. Don't fall for it! Have a back-up plan. A scripture, a song or even a war cry. When you are tempted to hop onto an emotional roller coaster, remember that it isn't worth the cost of the ticket.

Let nothing or no one steal your joy! Rebuke the devil and he will flee. "Satan, in Jesus' Name I rebuke you and the temptation to be distressed. I am at peace because I am loved by the Prince of Peace."

A Prayer to Move Forward

Today I pray over those who are stagnant and struggling. "I rebuke the spirit of laziness, and the laid-back attitude that is operating in your mindset. I come against the heaviness that is causing you to languish where you are. I pray now that you shake yourself and move forward and allow the joy of the Lord to overcome you and endow you with strength. In Jesus' Name, be free from oppression and depression. In Jesus' name, move forward with purpose and intent to obey the will of the Lord for you this day, this year and the rest of your life. Amen and AMEN!"

Healing from Abortion

Are you in need of healing from the pain of an abortion? Are you a male that has suffered from the loss of the opportunity to raise their seed because of abortion or guilt from participating in one?

When I was sixteen, I was taken by a "family friend" to have an abortion. It is one thing I deeply regretted for years. Even after salvation, I had that hole in my being of loss. I held a tormenting mental memorial every year of the date of the abortion and the date that abortion clinic gave me of the expected due date.

Even though Christ had forgiven me, I refused to forgive myself. I felt that I deserved to feel tormented by my selfish, foolish act and that I should suffer. Over the years I became a quitter. I made rash decisions frequently and out of my emotions. I felt that I didn't deserve too much happiness. I could handle a little success, a small promotion but I would always quit the job before I went too far up the ladder. I aborted almost every breakthrough opportunity I had to really be successful.

In August 2013, God had had enough. My eyes were opened through a Christian fiction novel I read about a woman who was doing the same thing I was doing. She wasn't allowing herself to love her children wholeheartedly because she felt she didn't deserve them. She had not pursued her gifts fully because she felt she didn't deserve a bright future when she had robbed her child of having any at all. I made up in my mind that I was going to let go of the daughter, (I felt it was a girl), I never had and fully give her and the possibility of her to Jesus.

I stood outside of a book signing event in San Antonio, Texas and with a balloon I had taken from the table and I let it go. As I released it I spoke to the spirit of that child and I said, "Goodbye, I love you." Now, I have no more feelings of condemnation.

I took them to Calvary and I left them there, under the blood. I am free to write about it today and to ask you, if the area of your life that needs maintenance is unforgiveness towards YOURSELF to pray this prayer WITH me:

"Lord, I confess that I have not fully received your grace for my abortion. I acknowledge that by attempting to punish myself through failure and quitting and not feeling worthy of the joy of salvation I devalue the price that you paid for my forgiveness. For this, I repent. Forgive me and help me to receive the fullness of your grace. Thank you Jesus, for dying on the cross for my abortion. Help me to remember that I am, through Jesus Christ, worthy of every good gift that comes from you. When I am tempted to self-sabotage, help me to remember that my debt is paid in full. You are my only hope. With the Holy Ghost, my present Help, I will do this no longer. In Jesus' name, Amen."

"I'm not rebellious, I am just strongly motivated by the word no."

April Dishon Barker

A Prophetic Declaration to Praise

I prophesy to the broken spirit that a mending is happening every time you praise and that which was sent to steal, kill and destroy you was unsuccessful! Your long-standing trail has ended and You will live to see the goodness of God in the land of the living. **Praise is the pathway to resurrection power. Praise and live.**

Praise causes faith to stir.
Praise causes fear to flee.
Praise causes God to move.
Praise causes the earth to yield blessings.
Praise multiplies favor.
Praise adds heaps of blessings to our lives.
Praise Him in it!
Praise Him through it!
Praise Him because today you are out of it!
If you receive this breakthrough, say
"I praise You Lord!"
Continue to Praise and Live!

God Says, "I Will Settle the Settlements."

For all of you who have money that is tied up in court, negotiations, paperwork, lazy lawyers, payday loans, bad decisions, faulty business deals, co-signing gone wrong and withheld inheritances, raises, bonuses, perks and benefits I decree and declare:

Believe you will receive the settling of the settlement as the Lord has spoken. God is settling the settlement in His own way and it will be much more than you could have ever thought. Here are some prophetic directives to follow in advance:

1. Write out the amount you need to pay off your personal debt. (Habakkuk 2:2)

2. Ask God for it. (Luke 11:9)

3. When it comes, pay your tithe and then pay off the debt, no matter how large. (Ecclesiastes 5:4-6)

4. Sow into a good ministry. (Galatians 6:7)

5. Sow into your legacy by saving some. (Proverbs 6:6-8)

"Lord, You are faithful to perform Your Words that have been spoken over us in prophecy, glimpsed by us in dreams and requested by us in prayer and petitions. You are faithful to perform Your Word. In the meantime, we wait patiently in the posture of prayer, praise and positive Biblical professions. Thank you for settling every settlement in our life. We shall have what we say and we shall learn to be quiet unless we are speaking life and blessing. In Jesus' Name, Amen and Amen!"

A Prayer for the Month of January & the New Year

May the Lord grant you the strength you need to transition into a better you.

May the spirit of discipline overtake your body and soul as you seek to make the changes necessary to thrive.

May the Lord light your path in a way that is undeniable.

May your decision making process be easy and without regrets.

May you trust in God and not man.

May you repent and not return to it.

May you flourish in all you say think and do.

May you be blessed all the days of your life as you bless the Lord in all circumstances.

May you be overwhelmed by the love of God!

A Shift in February

February will be the beginning of a season of shifting for many. To everything there is a season. A time. A purpose.

Many will enter into new seasons. Before you enter one door, you must properly close another or things and people may follow you that shouldn't. Make sure you know where you are going, who you are leading and who is leading you in this new season.

This shift will be the best shift you have ever lived. It will encompass better physical health, greater spiritual stamina and stability in finance coupled with implementation of disciplined budgeting. There is a purpose under heaven for this season. Stay under heaven's leading and you will walk wisely through the shift and be sustained in the season.

For some the shift will be short and sweet. For others, it will be a lengthy stroll.

For even less it will be your last season on earth. You will be sustained as you walk into your latter days and receive the greater that has been promised. Haggai 2:9

Take this promise and rejoice. The heart posture of rejoicing is what will determine the potency of your shift. How far you will go, how weighty His glory will rest on you and how heavy the blessing will be.

Praise God for the shift and in the shift and especially when you arrive to the place you are being shifted to.

Prophetic Declaration for the Month of March

March is a month of double blessing! I decree and declare that the month of March will be an amazing time of turnaround for you and your family! What was broken will be fixed. What was torn will be mended. What is missing will be found and what was lost shall be returned. It is a month of Double.

Double blessing in your prayer life.
Double blessing in your home.
Double blessing in your family.
Double blessing in your business.
Double blessing in your ministry.
Double blessing in your finance.
Double blessing in your prayer time.
Double blessing in your body.

Prophetic Declaration for the Month of April

This month you will receive the ultimate ROI (Return of Investment). Blessings will spring up from every avenue in which you have invested. Things that have "gone South" will turn North.

The theme of your life this month will be arise, increase and expand. What is dead will resurrect! What is low will increase and what has been a closed limited area will open and expand.

Your communication with your children will become clear and productive!

Your ministry will revive!

Your health will improve!

You will reap with joy in every area that you have sown in tears!

There will be six figure job offers given (pay your tithes).

There will be restoration of marriages (be ready for change).

There will be repentance from old friends (forgive and be forgiven).

There will be supernatural weight loss (prepare to maintain it).

There will be miraculous growth in ministries (go after the lost and increase prayer and fasting).

There will be double profits (in businesses that tithe and help the poor and needy).

God is saying ASK! ASK! ASK! and it shall be given.

What do you want? What is your desire? Ask.

THE HEAVENS ARE OPEN! HALLELUJAH!

Miracles in May

In this month many are weary and disappointed. That is the perfect time to believe God for miracles. Miracles are happening all around you. Ask God to show you them daily. When you increase your faith to believe God for miracles, you will not only see them, you will begin to experience them.

Do not allow your status, intellect, ability or pride stop you from receiving miracles and praying for them. Ask God for miracles everyday with the faith of a child and the expectation to receive them. May you see miracles every day.

A Prophetic Directive for June

This month, do all that you can to stay away from joy-killing thoughts, environments and people. Yes, the first five months have flashed by. You may not have done all that you said at the beginning of the year, but with each day is a new mercy and a new grace to "Get it done!"

I applaud your efforts thus far and am so proud of you. Would you take a moment to celebrate yourself? Think hard and share something amazing that God has blessed you to be able to accomplish. Then spend this month building on it and do even greater things to the glory of God!

Consistency is key. Increase your prayer time faithfully and consistently. Whatever you do this month, do it with JOY!

A Joyful July!

This July will be full of Joy.
You will:
SHOUT for Joy!
LEAP with Joy!
SING with Joy!
Make JOYFUL confessions!
This will be a GROUNDBREAKING month! As you step out in obedience, God will cause the ground to break open for you!

Your dances of praise will cause the breaking open to be deep and fast! Praise Him, Praise Him, Praise Him!

You will not be put to shame. You will be put to SHOUT!

Your Praise will OPEN DOORS!

You will be given a SECOND CHANCE to SHOW UP WELL!

You will SHAKE OFF timidity and STAND UP in your talents!

Your gift has made room for you!

CONGRATULATIONS!

Changes will be signs of God's greater plan. WELCOME CHANGE!

Get ready to say farewell. Farewell to old seasons and assignments that served you well and where you served well. Time to GRADUATE! (YES, THIS IS YOUR RELEASE!)

(YES, BECAUSE YOU ASKED FOR CONFIRMATION!)

Joy is your portion.

Joy is your right.

Joy is your future.

Joy is yours forever.

Watch God respond to your Joyfulness with ABUNDANCE!

Happy Birthday to the JOYFUL you! Shift into your newness, shift into consistent joy and confidant jubilation.

New levels of JOY and new opportunity come with this lifestyle.

Welcome to the Joy of the Lord! Stay here, don't go back.

"Lord, thank you for Groundbreaking Joy being implanted into our hearts, minds and souls as we receive this fresh impartation of Joy. Thank you for yoke-destroying anointing being poured out over all that we say because of our joyful stance. We shift into Joy, we sit into joyful positions, we stand in joyful places, we rest in joyful homes and dance in joyful celebration. In Jesus' Name, Amen."

An August of Accountability, Adjustment & Alignment

As we maintain our joyful foundation and daily disposition and move into action, we remember that it daily starts with us. We take accountability. We will:

Mature in our mindset.
Make tough decisions and come out of double-mindedness.
Accept Responsibility for our inactions and take action.
Adjust to the new level with grace and ease.
Align ourselves with the Word of God and be free from conformity.

Here are three prophetic directives:

1. Take Accountability- the fact or condition of being accountable; required or expected to justify actions or decisions. Evaluate where you are hindering your growth spiritually, physically, mentally, and financially. Then,

2. Make Adjustment- a small alteration or movement made to achieve a desired fit, appearance, or result. Erase and eradicate excuses and do the opposite. Ex. if you are overspending, stop immediately and go on a

no spend month. If you are being negative, take a vow of silence unless the words you speak are life, blessing and positive. If you are unhealthy start today getting moving. Fast from fast food and putting things in your body that corrode and corrupt it. If you are spiritually dead and/or dying, get up and go to church every Sunday for the rest of the year and go to the altar. JESUS is waiting for you! Lastly,

3. Make Alignment- in correct or appropriate relative positions. A position of agreement or alliance. Carefully and prayerfully get into the right posture spiritually. Pray, fast, read your Bible, connect with your church community. All of it! Humble yourselves and repent from all compromise. Jesus is coming soon!

God is calling His people into leadership, entrepreneurship, and positions of authority in every sphere. Shake off fear and laziness and prepare for more responsibility and productivity.

Mentally- study, read and train. God's Word AND, autobiographies, take trainings, read books on where you are going, learn new things.

Financially- save AND sow. I challenge you, give to someone you know is living right and doing the work of the Lord. When you get paid, give your tithe, save a tenth and give as you feel led to a cause or an individual who is blessing your life. It will come back to you.

As we do these things and think positive and powerful thoughts, we can expect doors of opportunity and windows of blessing to open up to us. We will not be where we are today, this time next month if we take action in August!

Ready, Set, Grow, Go!

"Lord, thank you for the charge to build on the joyful foundation of life you have given us. We accept accountability for our actions and inactivity. We make the necessary adjustments. Help us get into alignment to receive directions, corrections, open doors and many blessings and opportunities. With our hands lifted up and our mouths filled with praise, we bless thee Oh Lord and we say yes and amen, in Jesus' Name!

Sow in September

September is a month of sowing seed. You will see a harvest as you plant the seed and speak to what you are planting. Watch and praise!

Sow- to plant the seeds of (a plant or crop).
Sow to your local church.
Sow to your parents.
Sow to that teacher who made your education meaningful.
Sow to that coach who pushed you to be your best.
Sow to the ministries/ministers who have blessed your life.
Sow into your future. (Savings)
Sow into your spouse.
Sow into your education.
Sow into your discipleship.
Sow into your healing.

You Will Overcome in October

Your ears are wide open now to hear the truth and you will not move forward in fear but in faith. The supernatural provision of the Lord is going to begin to show up for you in tangible ways and you will be amazed at His favor and blessings. Your personal prayer and devotion time is about to extend, and you will see great results of peace of mind when you prioritize this discipline.

You are entering into a higher understanding of praise as a weapon. It confuses the onslaught of depression. As you purposefully praise God this month, you will experience levels of joy that you have never seen or felt. Your emotions will bow to the inhabitation of God's presence that will overwhelm your heart, home, and personal space as you cultivate the truth of God's worthiness.

You will be free from all addiction as you focus on the study of God's Word. Unplug and tune into a different program, one of prayer and study. For those of you who received and acknowledged the shift that took place in your life in the last season, do not be scared in this new place. Perfect love casts out fear and you will be supplied with everything you need to succeed.

There is no lack in God, there is no laziness in God. Get up and declare your victory! When you can't move praise with your lips. When you can't speak, praise with your thoughts. Dance daily in praise and thanksgiving of your overcoming. Develop your dance. Practice praise until it is a part of your natural response to life. Be a praise warrior!

This is how you will OVERCOME in OCTOBER and beyond!

A Yes in November

Yes Lord.
Yes to Your will!
Yes to Your way!
Yes to Your plan!
Yes to what You say!
Yes when I want to say no.
Yes when I don't feel like saying yes.
Yes to gratitude.
Yes Lord.

You Will Have a Deliberate December

We have all experienced circumstances in the last couple of years that we have never felt before, seen before, or heard about before. Instead of waiting until January to fast, pray and seek the Lord, let's do so now. May I suggest that you commit to taking at least a day out of your week for the next four weeks and do a water-only fast? Instead of eating food, open your Bible and eat the Word.

Might I encourage you to take a week and use no electronics? Immerse yourself in His presence. Instead of being addicted to Social Media Communities, get accustomed to the communion of the Holy Spirit. If you wait until January to hear from the Lord, YOU WILL MISS out on so much that He wants to do in this month.

"Lord,

I confess that I have not been as deliberate as I could in staying connected to You and I am sorry. Please help me to be deliberate in my time with you in personal devotion. Restore to me the JOY of my SALVATION. Renew my fervor for You, Your Presence, Your Word, Your house and Your call on my life this month, in the coming year and for the rest of my life.

In Jesus' name,

Amen!"

Basic Steps of Forgiveness

This Sunday School teaching has revolutionized my life and most specifically my heart.

Basic Steps of Forgiveness:

1. Guard your heart immediately after an incident.
2. Seek God's help and ask Him to heal your wounds.
3. Start praying for the well-being of the offender.
4. As much as possible, don't dwell on the incident.
5. Relinquish all rights of the offense to God.
6. Realize Jesus had more right than anyone to hold a grudge, but He still forgave. We must do no less.
7. Realize the actual offense against you was specifically paid for on the cross. It has been dealt with and we must act on that fact.

It doesn't matter if you are right or wrong in a conflict. If you hold resentment, bitterness, or anger toward another party, you are sinning. More importantly, you are crippling yourself spiritually and rendering yourself ineffective.

These notes are from a handout I received to prepare to teach a Sunday School lesson in July 2015 at First Baptist Church, San Andres while on San Andres Diaspora. I do not know the original author, but these notes have blessed my life and I teach them regularly to others. I pray they bless you as much as they have blessed me.

Every day make it your business to apologize, forgive and repeat.

A Prophetic Declaration of Promotion

I prophesy this morning that you will endure the process of promotion. That you will face your fear today and rebuke it. There is no GOOD THING that God withholds from those who walk upright. Accept the things He has not allowed yet as not good for you right now and trust His love and His timing.

God's love never fails! God's decisions are always right.

Therefore, you will seek HIM before you make decisions so that you will remain upright.

You will seek Him before you speak to 'them' and remain upright.

You will be honest with your shortcomings and stop making excuses for your disobedience and remain upright.

You will speak victory and not defeat over your family, finances, and your future for it is the heritage of the saints.

Receive today God as your sun, your light, your lifter, your protector, your provider.

Receive His grace to make the necessary changes in your heart and head in order to walk upright at all times in Jesus' Name, Amen.

The Lord God is a sun and shield and gives grace and glory: no good thing will He withhold from them that walk uprightly.

A Prophetic Declaration of Productivity

I prophesy today that you will have great productivity. The spirit of procrastination shall not hinder your progress. You will be diligent in business and successful in accomplishing all that you set out to do. You will complete your to-do list as you complete each task with the leading of the Holy Spirit.

Do not dread tough conversations, God's mercy has already made peace in the hearts of your enemies and every right has been made wrong. EVERY RIGHT HAS BEEN MADE WRONG. While you were sleep, God was dealing with the heart of the King and has turned the ruling of that situation in your favor. In Jesus' Name.

Receive the recompense that is due you and be humble when accepting the apology that is coming your way. Let the Holy Ghost of God allow grace and forgiveness to rule your tongue today in Jesus' Name.

A Prophetic Declaration of Progress

I prophesy tonight that you are not regressing out of the glory of God!

You will not lose ground.

Physical manifestation is here and no demon in hell can stop it.

The enemy is confused, and you are not in Jesus' Name.

The devil is defeated, and you are not, in Jesus' name.

The shift did happen, and nothing can change it.

Keep praising, keep moving forward and keep declaring victory, especially in the places where you don't see it.

We walk by FAITH and NOT by sight!

Whatever you do, keep walking.

Let Go So You Can Grow

You CANNOT hold on to the old and also grab ahold of the new at the same time.

I prophesy that you will let go of that anger, you will let go of that fear, you will let go of that regret, you will let go of that pain and disappointment. God is already handing you the recompense and restoration.

Open your hands and receive it. Stop looking back and reaching back. See what lies ahead, then grab ahold of it. Let go of your past and latch on to your future. I prophesy now that your new assignment is about to begin. God will hide you so He can heal you. When the healing is complete, He will send you. Get ready to Go!

Other Books by the Author

Non-Fiction:
"Nuggets for the 21 Day Fast"
"Nuggets for the New Believer"

Christian Fiction:
The "What About" Series Co-Authored with Michelle Stimpson
"What About Momma's House?"
"What About Love?"
What About Tomorrow?"

April Dishon Barker's God-given mission is to proclaim God's Word through Psalm, Pen, Preaching, Prophecy and Prayer with Joy. Stay connected:

For Speaking Engagements email: iamaprilbarker@gmail.com

For Flourish Walk Sessions email: flourishwalk@gmail.com

YouTube: Flourish in Prayer

Insta: @flourishwalk

Facebook: Flourish Walk

Website: www.flourishwalk.org

Front and back cover Photo Credit: The Look Creator's Studio

http://www.legendarylookinteriors.com/studio

Made in the USA
Middletown, DE
20 October 2022

13149143R00050